Published by Creative Education
and Creative Paperbacks
P.O. Box 227, Mankato, Minnesota 56002
Creative Education and Creative Paperbacks
are imprints of The Creative Company
www.thecreativecompany.us

Design by The Design Lab
Production by Joe Kahnke
Art direction by Rita Marshall
Printed in the United States of America

Photographs by Alamy (WaterFrame), Corbis (Norbert
Wu/Science Faction), Dreamstime (Cigdem Sean
Cooper, Piers Diment, Serban Enache, Idpeacev,
Steven Melanson, Nicholasrexrode, Planctonvideo,
Ricok, Julija Sapic, Typhoonski, Aizhong Wang),
Flickr (Mandie)

Library of Congress Cataloging-in-Publication Data
Bodden, Valerie.
Jellyfish / Valerie Bodden.
p. cm. — (Amazing animals)
Summary: A basic exploration of the appearance,
behavior, and habitat of jellyfish, the bell-shaped,
oceanic invertebrates. Also included is a story from
folklore explaining why jellyfish have squishy bodies.
Includes bibliographical references and index.
ISBN 978-1-60818-755-3 (hardcover)
ISBN 978-1-62832-363-4 (pbk)
ISBN 978-1-56660-797-1 (eBook)
1. Jellyfish—Juvenile literature. I. Title. II. Series:
Amazing animals.
QL377.S4 B63 2017
593.5/3—dc23 2016004788

CCSS: RI.1.1, 2, 4, 5, 6, 7; RI.2.2, 5, 6, 7, 10;
RI.3.1, 5, 7, 8; RF.1.1, 3, 4; RF.2.3, 4

HC 9 8 7 6 5
PBK 9 8 7 6 5 4 3 2 1

AMAZING ANIMALS

JELLYFISH

BY VALERIE BODDEN

CREATIVE EDUCATION · CREATIVE PAPERBACKS

Jellyfish are bell-shaped sea animals. They have no bones, blood, or brain. There are about 200 kinds of true jellies in the world.

Animals without backbones, like jellyfish, are called invertebrates

Some jellies have four arms that hang down from the mouth

Many jellyfish have clear bodies. But some jellies are pink, orange, blue, or red. Many give off a blue or green glow. Long **tentacles** (*TEN-tuh-culz*) hang from the body. The tentacles can sting.

tentacles bendy limbs

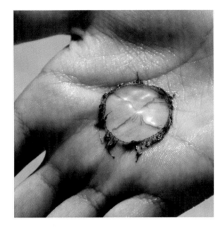

The smallest jellies are the size of your thumb. But the biggest can be six feet (1.8 m) across. The tentacles of some jellyfish can reach more than 100 feet (30.5 m). That's longer than a basketball court!

The lion's mane jellyfish (opposite) is the largest known kind of jelly

*Jellies that live in
dark waters can often
make their own light*

Jellyfish live in all the world's **oceans**. Many jellyfish love warm water. Others live in deep, cold parts of the ocean.

oceans big areas of deep, salty water

Jellies use their arms to bring food into the mouth

Jellyfish will eat almost anything they catch in their tentacles. Their favorite foods are **plankton**, shrimp, crabs, and small fish. Some even eat other jellyfish!

plankton tiny plants and animals that float in the oceans and other bodies of water

*A polyp feeds for weeks
before it changes shape*

Jellyfish
start life as an egg. The egg falls to the seafloor. It becomes a **polyp** (*POL-ip*). The polyp is tube-shaped and grows tiny tentacles. After a few weeks, the polyp splits into small pieces. Each of these pieces becomes a baby jellyfish. Most jellyfish live a year or less. But a few kinds of jellies can live up to 30 years.

polyp a tube-shaped animal with a mouth surrounded by small tentacles

Some animals eat jellyfish bells, but sea turtles eat the whole jelly

Jellyfish

squeeze their bell-shaped body to move. But they don't get very far that way. Mostly, jellies are carried on the oceans' **currents**. Sometimes thousands of jellyfish drift near each other. They are easy for **predators** to catch. Sea turtles, sharks, and tuna like to eat jellies.

currents the movement of ocean water

predators animals that kill and eat other animals

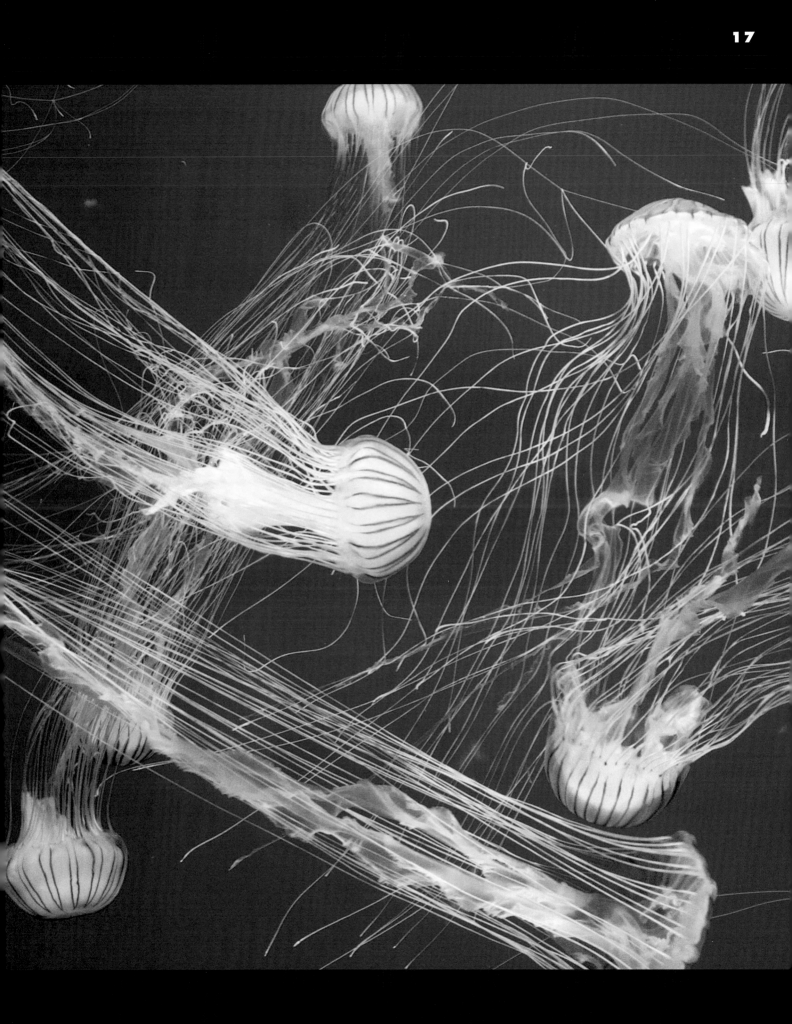

Storms at sea often wash jellies onto beaches. A jellyfish cannot move on the beach. But sometimes its tentacles can still sting.

*A cannonball
jellyfish on the beach
is usually harmless*

Some people keep small jellyfish as pets. Pet jellies need a lot of care. Other people see jellyfish in zoos or at the beach. It is fun to watch these sea animals float in the water!

Beautiful jellyfish are some of Earth's most mysterious animals

A Jellyfish Story

Why do jellyfish have squishy bodies? People in Japan told a story about this. They said Jellyfish once had long legs, shiny scales, and a strong shell. One day, the Queen of the Sea invited some animals to a party. She secretly wanted to steal parts of their bodies for herself. Jellyfish told the other animals about her plan. The Queen was so mad that she took away Jellyfish's legs, scales, and shell.

Read More

Herriges, Ann. *Jellyfish*. Minneapolis: Bellwether Media, 2007.

West, David. *Tide Pool Animals*. North Mankato, Minn.: Smart Apple Media, 2014.

Websites

Enchanted Learning: Jellyfish
http://www.enchantedlearning.com/subjects/invertebrates/jellyfish
/Jellyfishcoloring.shtml
This site has jellyfish facts and a picture to print and color.

Ranger Rick: Jellyfish
https://www.nwf.org/Kids/Ranger-Rick/Animals/Fish/Jellyfish.aspx
This site has facts, diagrams, and pictures of jellyfish.

Note: Every effort has been made to ensure that the websites listed above are suitable for children, that they have educational value, and that they contain no inappropriate material. However, because of the nature of the Internet, it is impossible to guarantee that these sites will remain active indefinitely or that their contents will not be altered.

Index